DISCOVER DOGS WITH THE AMERICAN CANINE ASSOCIATION

I LIKE PIT BULLS!

Linda Bozzo

It is the Mission of the American Canine Association (ACA) to provide registered dog owners with the educational support needed for raising, training, showing, and breeding the healthiest pets expected by responsible pet owners throughout the world. Through our activities and services, we encourage and support the dog world in order to promote best-known husbandry standards as well as to ensure that the voice and needs of our customers are quickly and properly addressed.

Our continued support, commitment, and direction are guided by our customers, including veterinary, legal, and legislative advisors. ACA aims to provide the most efficient, cooperative, and courteous service to our customers and strives to set the standard for education and problem solving for all who depend on our services.

For more information, please visit www.acacanines.com, e-mail customerservice@acadogs.com, phone 1-800-651-8332, or write to the American Canine Association at PO Box 121107, Clermont, FL 34712.

Published in 2017 by Enslow Publishing, LLC.
101 W. 23rd Street, Suite 240, New York, NY 10011

Library of Congress Cataloging-in-Publication Data
Names: Bozzo, Linda, author.
Title: I like pit bulls! / Linda Bozzo.
Description: New York, NY : Enslow Publishing, 2017. | Series: Discover dogs with the American Canine Association | Includes bibliographical references and index. | Audience: Ages 5 and up. | Audience: Grades K to 3.
Identifiers: LCCN 2016020289| ISBN 9780766081598 (library bound) | ISBN 9780766081574 (pbk.) | ISBN 9780766081581 (6-pack)
Subjects: LCSH: Pit bull terriers—Juvenile literature.
Classification: LCC SF429.P58 B69 2017 | DDC 636.755/9--dc23
LC record available at https://lccn.loc.gov/2016020289

Printed in China

To Our Readers: We have done our best to make sure all websites in this book were active and appropriate when we went to press. However, the author and the publisher have no control over and assume no liability for the material available on those websites or on any websites they may link to. Any comments or suggestions can be sent by e-mail to customerservice@enslow.com.

Photo Credits: Cover, p. 1 adogslifephoto/iStock/Thinkstock; p. 3 (left) Danita Delimont/Gallo Images/Getty Images; p. 3 (right) Tom Myers/Shutterstock.com; p. 5 © iStockphoto.com/IsaacLKoval; p. 6 dezi/Shutterstock.com; p. 9 JenD/E+/Getty Images; p. 10 Zann Goff/EyeEm/Getty Images; p. 13 (left) ruthlessphotos.com/Moment Open/Getty Images; p 13 (right) © iStockphoto.com/jclegg (collar), Luisa Leal Photography/Shutterstock.com (bed), gvictoria/Shutterstock.com (brush), In-Finity/Shutterstock.com (dishes), © iStockphoto.com/Lisa Thornberg (leash, toys); p. 14 Roberto A Sanchez/E+/Getty Images; p. 15 Tannis Toohey/Toronto Star/Getty Images; p. 17 princessdlaf/E+/Getty Images; p. 18 Corbis/VCG/Getty Images; p. 19 The Washington Post/Getty Images; p. 21 360b/Shutterstock.com; p. 22 InBetweentheBlinks/Shutterstock.com.

Enslow Publishing
101 W. 23rd Street
Suite 240
New York, NY 10011
USA
enslow.com

CONTENTS

IS A PIT BULL RIGHT FOR YOU?

Well-trained pit bulls can be great family pets. If you do not have other pets, a pit bull might be right for you.

This breed is not recommended for first-time dog owners.

A DOG OR A PUPPY?

Pit bulls love to learn. Training must start as soon as you bring this puppy home. If you do not have time to train a puppy, another kind of dog may be better for your family.

Pit bulls grow to be medium to large in size.

Pit bulls may need special training classes.

LOVING YOUR PIT BULL

Show your pit bull lots of love. Teach him tricks. Give him toys to play with.

This breed is believed to come from different bull and terrier types.

EXERCISE

Pit bulls need lots of exercise every day. Games like **fetch** and long walks on a **leash** are a must for these pups. These dogs like to dig and climb! They need a yard with a high fence to play in.

Pit bulls are very strong dogs.

FEEDING YOUR PIT BULL

Dogs can be fed wet or dry dog food. Ask a **veterinarian (vet)**, a doctor for animals, which food is best for your dog and how much to feed her.

Give your pit bull fresh, clean water every day.

Remember to keep your dog's food and water dishes clean. Dirty dishes can make a dog sick.

Do not feed your dog people food. It can make her sick.

Your new dog will need:

a collar with a tag

a bed

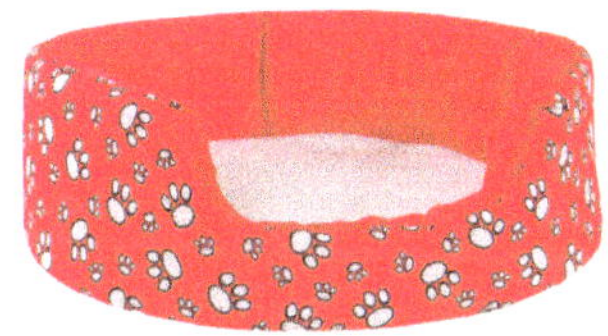

a brush

food and water dishes

a leash

toys

GROOMING

Use a gentle soap made just for dogs.

Pit bulls **shed**. This means their short hair falls out. Brushing your pit bull will help keep him clean and looking his best.

Your dog will need a bath every so often. A pit bull's nails need to be clipped. A vet or **groomer** can show you how. Your dog's ears should be cleaned and his teeth should be brushed by an adult.

WHAT YOU SHOULD KNOW ABOUT PIT BULLS

This breed does not always get along with other pets. They can be great with kids, but adult pit bulls are very strong and should be watched carefully with small children.

Pit bulls are banned in some places.

Pit bulls are hunters. They should be kept away from other small animals, both indoors and outdoors.

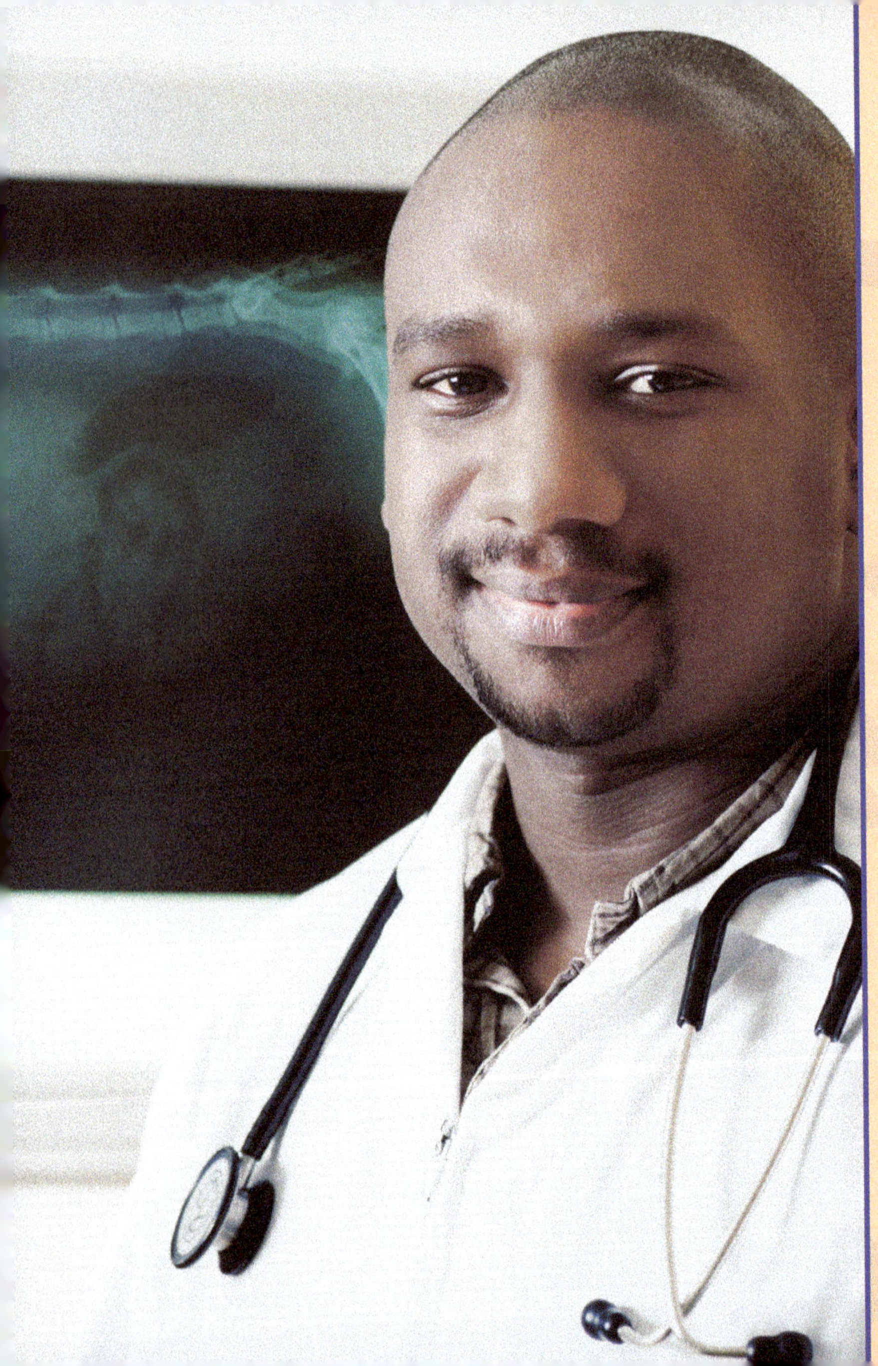

You will need to take your new dog to the vet for a checkup. He will need shots, called **vaccinations**, and yearly checkups to keep him healthy. If you think your dog may be sick or hurt, call your vet.

A GOOD FRIEND

Pit bulls can live more than 10 years. This means you and your friend can spend a long, happy life together.

If cared for properly, pit bulls can be loyal family members.

NOTE TO PARENTS

It is important to consider having your dog spayed or neutered when the dog is young. Spaying and neutering are operations that prevent unwanted puppies and can help improve the overall health of your dog.

It is also a good idea to microchip your dog, in case he or she gets lost. A vet will implant a microchip under the skin containing an identification number that can be scanned at a vet's office or animal shelter. The microchip registry is contacted and the company uses the ID number to look up your information from a database.

Some towns require licenses for dogs, so be sure to check with your town clerk.

For more information, speak with a vet.

There are many dogs, young and old, waiting to be adopted from animal shelters and rescue groups.

Words to Know

fetch To go after a toy and bring it back.

groomer A person who bathes and brushes dogs.

leash A chain or strap that attaches to the dog's collar.

shed When dog hair falls out so new hair can grow.

vaccinations Shots that dogs need to stay healthy.

veterinarian (vet) A doctor for animals.

Read About Dogs

Books

Mattern, Joanne. *All About Pit Bulls.* North Mankato, MN: Capstone Press, 2013.

Wittrock, Jeni. *American Pit Bull Terriers.* Edina, MN: ABDO Publishing Company, 2012.

Websites

American Canine Association Inc., Kids Corner
acakids.com
Visit the official website of the American Canine Association.

National Geographic for Kids, Pet Central
kids.nationalgeographic.com/explore/pet-central/
Learn more about dogs and other pets at the official site of the National Geographic Society for Kids.

INDEX